Do good and share?
— Teri Davidson

Presented to

_____

By

_____

Occasion

_____

Princess Hannavas

and the

Blackberry Bully

Teri Davidson

Illustrated by Lydia Davis

Princess Hannavas and the Blackberry Bully
© 2020 Text by Teri Davidson
© 2020 Illustrations by Lydia Davis

BOOK VILLAGES and the BOOK VILLAGES logo are registered trademarks of Book Villages. Absence of ® in connection with marks of Book Villages or other parties does not indicate an absence of registration of those marks.

ISBN: 978-1-94429-874-6

Cover and Interior Design by Niddy Griddy Design, Inc.

Holy Bible, New International Version®, NIV® Copyright ©1973, 1978, 1984, 2011 by Biblica, Inc.® Used by permission. All rights reserved worldwide.

LCCN: 2020923197

Printed in the United States of America

1 2 3 4 5 6 7 8 9 10 Printing / Year 26 25 24 23 22 21 20

For Savannah and John,
Together you created Princess Hannavas' adventures.
Thank you for letting me share her stories.

And for AJ, who isn't afraid of spiders.

Princess Hannavas lives in a castle in the magical land of Tuneep. She lives with her momma, the Queen, King Daddy, and her brother, Prince Bubby.

Princess Hannavas LOVES blackberries!
And she loves to go blackberry picking in
her Daddy's garden.

She will pick one and eat one, pick one and eat one.

When she gathers a whole basket,
the Queen will make a cobbler.

Hannavas can carry three
whole baskets at a time!

One day, Hannavas was frightened to find a very angry-looking spider hiding in her blackberries.

"Why are you eating my blackberries?" asked the spider.

"These are not your blackberries, they are MY blackberries," said Princess Hannavas. "This is my daddy's garden. He is the King."

The spider said, "Everyone knows King Daddy's blackberries are magical. That's why I'm stealing them. They'll make me strong."

Princess Hannavas told the spider, "The blackberries aren't magical. They make you strong because they are a fruit and eating fruit makes you healthy."

But the spider was a bully and he didn't care who the blackberries really belonged to or why they made him strong. He just wanted them all to himself. He said, "Give them to me Hannavas, or I'll BITE you!"

Princess Hannavas was very scared. But just then she heard Clip, Clop, Clip, Clop, Neigh . . . .

It was Prince Bubby galloping in on his trusty horse.

Prince Bubby knew the princess was afraid of spiders and he could see that the Blackberry Bully Spider was being especially mean.

So, Prince Bubby jumped down off his horse and ran over and scooped up the spider. He spun him around, and spun him around, and THREW the spider into the lake!

Princess Hannavas was so happy to be rid of that spider that she gave Prince Bubby a BIG hug. Together, they returned to the castle.

Hannavas learned a lesson that day from the mean, selfish spider.

She invited all of her friends and the people of Tuneep to her castle to share the cobblers she had helped her momma bake.

But while her friends enjoyed their dessert, Hannavas kept thinking about that spider.

She wondered why he was so mean to her.
Maybe someone had been mean to him first.

Maybe they told him he was too short or not good at playing sports and that's why the spider wanted the blackberries to make him strong. Maybe that poor spider just really needed someone to show him kindness.

Hannavas made a big bowl of the yummy blackberry cobbler and took it outside to share with the spider. The spider was grateful for the cobbler.

He was also very surprised Hannavas would be nice to him, even after he scared her.

Hannavas told the spider she forgave him, and the spider promised never to bully anyone ever again.

"And do not forget to do good and to share with others, for with such sacrifices God is pleased."

Hebrews 13:16 (NIV)

When our daughter was a very little girl, she preferred for my husband to tuck her into bed. Every night, Savannah (that's Hannavas spelled backward) and her daddy would make up bedtime stories that starred characters based on our family and usually a stuffed animal or two.

Savannah's favorite story was about a mean spider that Princess Hannavas found in the blackberry patch. She memorized the story and repeated it for years. We have very sweet memories surrounding this story.

In the spring of 2020, I asked Savannah if she and her daddy would be okay if I turned their short little bedtime story into a children's book. They agreed, and I began the very exciting journey of writing my first book. What I didn't anticipate was how amazing it would be when completed. I owe credit for that to Lydia Davis. Lydia, your illustrations are stunning! Thank you for bringing our family bedtime story to life so beautifully!

I hope all who read it enjoy the story as much as we have.

Easy Blackberry Cobbler

4 cups blackberries, fresh or frozen
1 Tablespoon lemon juice
1 large egg
1 cup all-purpose flour
1 cup sugar
1/2 cup chopped pecans
6 Tablespoons butter, melted

1) Preheat oven to 375 degrees. Place the blackberries in a greased 8" x 8" pan; sprinkle with the lemon juice.

2) Stir together the egg, sugar, and flour in a bowl until mixture resembles coarse meal.

3) Sprinkle this mixture over the fruit. Sprinkle the pecans over the last layer. Drizzle melted butter over the topping.

4) Bake for 30 to 35 minutes or until slightly browned and bubbly. Let stand 10 minutes before serving.

To order additional copies of this book,
or to contact Teri Davidson, go to
www.princesshannavas.com.